SHAGGY DOG EATS!

SHAGGY DOG EATS!

30 RECIPES FOR EASY, DELICIOUS DOG TREATS

Christy Bright

STERLING
New York

STERLING
New York

An Imprint of Sterling Publishing
1166 Avenue of the Americas
New York, NY 10036

ISBN 978-1-4549-1888-2

Distributed in Canada by Sterling Publishing Co., Inc.
c/o Canadian Manda Group, 664 Annette Street
Toronto, Ontario, Canada M6S 2C8
Distributed in the United Kingdom by GMC Distribution Services
Castle Place, 166 High Street, Lewes, East Sussex, England BN7 1XU
Distributed in Australia by Capricorn Link (Australia) Pty. Ltd.
P.O. Box 704, Windsor, NSW 2756, Australia

For information about custom editions, special sales, and premium and corporate purchases, please contact Sterling Special Sales at 800-805-5489 or specialsales@sterlingpublishing.com.

Manufactured in China

2 4 6 8 10 9 7 5 3 1

www.sterlingpublishing.com

Interior Design by Amy Trombat

CONTENTS

INTRODUCTION

This story did not start with a Doggie Treat Cookbook.

It started with a love of shelter dogs and stray dogs and many volunteer hours spent at a rural animal shelter in Roanoke, Texas. After college, I worked a short time in a veterinarian office and then spent many hours in the obedience ring and hunt test arena with a big goofy chocolate Labrador named Ruger. Nutrition was always important. I can remember many conversations with other dog handlers about what brand of dog food was highest in protein, what food gave a dog the best coat, and what food helped keep a dog at a good weight. My grandmother always fed table scraps to her dogs, and I always fed mine kibble.

Two worlds have since collided, and if you fast-forward to today, science has gotten involved and the pendulum has shifted. Once table scraps were taboo and responsible dog owners fed dogs only kibble, but now I see a shift to whole foods and lean proteins for our animals, especially in light of all the big food brand recalls. Maybe we trusted big companies too much. Maybe there was something to what my grandmother fed her dogs. I believe it goes back to the wise saying "Everything in moderation."

Shaggy Dog Eats! is packed with very simple easy-to-follow recipes. Almost all the ingredients can be substituted for. If your dog has a grain allergy, just substitute quinoa flour, buckwheat flour, chickpea flour, or spelt flour. Many of these ingredients can be found in larger grocery stores or bought through large online stores. Do you have a senior dog that needs a softer treat? Then cut down the cooking time. If you want a treat to come out crispier, cook it longer. The protein sources also can be interchanged depending on the preferred diet you feed your dog.

Every recipe published in this book has been researched and developed in my kitchen. Every treat has been taste tested by a very picky goldendoodle, an eat-anything beagle, a cat who thinks she is a dog, and an 11-year-old. Yes, all my recipes are "human grade," and my son has been known to eat a few.

The great thing about cooking for dogs is that they never complain! So have some fun in the kitchen. Let your kids learn to cook, host bake sales that raise money for local shelters, or just enjoy the feeling you get when you "know" where the food you give your dogs comes from because the tail wags are so worth it!

Ingredients to Avoid

Some ingredients that should *never* be included in dog treats:

Onions*

Raisins and grapes

Coffee and caffeine

Avocados

Yeast dough

Xylitol

Rhubarb

Macadamia nuts

Corn on the cob

Fatty foods

Chocolate**

*Garlic is part of the onion family but can be given in small amounts. Garlic has been thought to help ward off fleas. Give garlic only when it is cooked into treats, never raw.

**Carob chips are a great substitute for chocolate. Carob chips are made from the pod of a carob tree. Carob is less bitter than chocolate and has a natural sweetness.

Easy Peasy Treats

ingredients :

2 cups (473 ml) wheat germ

3 (2.5 oz [71 g]) jars chicken and broth baby food

2 tablespoons (30 ml) water

1 Preheat oven to 350°F (177°C). In a medium bowl mix together wheat germ, baby food, and water. You may need to add more water, but the dough should be crumbly.

2 Knead the dough into a ball and roll it out onto a lightly floured surface (I used whole wheat flour to lightly flour my surface) about ¼" (6.3 mm) thick. Cut into desired shapes. Line a cookie sheet with parchment paper and cook for about 15 minutes. You want the treats to be brown, firm, and crisp.

3 Store the treats in an airtight container for up to 2 weeks or freeze.

No Bake Snacks

ingredients :

½ cup (118 ml) milk

1 cup (237 ml) peanut butter

3 cups (710 ml) rolled oats

1 In a large bowl, combine the first 2 ingredients. Slowly stir in the oats. The mixture will be very thick.

2 Use a scooper or spoon to portion out the dough. Then roll into a uniform ball shape. Place on a cookie sheet lined with parchment paper. Place in the refrigerator for about 1 hour before serving so they can set up.

3 Store in an airtight container in the refrigerator for about 3 weeks or freeze for up to 3 months.

Savory Bones

ingredients :

2½ cups (591 ml) wheat flour

½ cup (118 ml) powdered dry milk

½ teaspoon (2.5 ml) salt

1 teaspoon (5 ml) brown sugar

6 tablespoons (89 ml) butter

1 egg, beaten

½ cup (118 ml) ice water

1 Preheat oven to 350°F (177°C).

2 Combine first 4 dry ingredients. Then cut in the butter with a pastry cutter until mealy. Mix in beaten egg. Add the ice water slowly until mixture forms a ball. Roll out on a floured surface about ¼" (6.3 mm) thick and cut into desired shapes. Bake for 25–35 minutes. Store in an airtight container for up to 3 weeks or freeze.

Beefy Bones

ingredients :

2 cups (473 ml) whole wheat flour

½ cup (118 ml) oats

A pinch of salt

1 egg

½ cup (118 ml) hot beef broth

¼ cup (59 ml) peanut butter

1 Preheat oven to 350°F (176°C). Combine all ingredients in a bowl and knead until you have formed a nice ball of dough (you can add a little water or broth if the dough is too dry). Roll the dough out on a floured surface about ¼" (6.3 mm) thick. Cut into bite-size squares or use cookie cutter shapes.

2 Lightly grease a cookie sheet and bake for about 30 minutes or until they become hard and crunchy. Cool completely and store in an airtight container for up to 3 weeks or freeze.

Sweet Potato Crunch

ingredients :

2 cups (473 ml) mashed sweet potatoes (about 2 sweet potatoes with skin on)

2 cups (473 ml) steel cut oats

¼ cup (59 ml) molasses

1 Cut up the sweet potatoes with the skin on and boil until soft. Drain and mash the sweet potatoes. Add the steel cut oats and molasses. Mix well.

2 Portion the mixture into bite-size dollops and place in a food dehydrator for approximately 8 hours or until they are nice and crunchy. You also can cook in an oven at a low temperature, 200°F (93°C), for about 6–8 hours.

3 Store in an airtight container for up to 3 weeks in the refrigerator or freeze.

Bacon! Bacon! Bacon!

ingredients :

1½ cups (355 ml) whole wheat flour

1 cup (237 ml) all-purpose flour

1 cup (237 ml) skim milk powder

⅓ cup (79 ml) bacon drippings (about 1 pound of bacon cooked)

1 large egg

1 cup (237 ml) cold water

1 Preheat oven to 300°F (149℃).

2 Combine both flours and milk powder in a large bowl. Drizzle with bacon drippings. Add egg and cold water. Mix well to form the dough (if the dough is too sticky, add flour until it reaches a suitable consistency for rolling). Turn the dough out onto a lightly floured surface. Roll the dough out to about ½" (12.8 mm) in thickness. Cut out shapes with cookie cutters and prick to prevent puffing. Place on an ungreased baking sheet and bake for 60 minutes. Makes about 3 dozen cookies, depending on size of shapes.

3 Store in an airtight container for up to 3 weeks in the refrigerator or freeze.

Hot Dog Crisps

ingredients :

2 hot dogs, chicken or turkey

1 Thinly slice hot dogs uniformly (about ⅛" [3.2 mm] thick). Place the slices on a microwave-safe plate. Try not to let the slices touch. Place a paper towel on top of the slices to help prevent any splattering.

2 Microwave on high for 2 minutes. Separate any slices that get stuck together and pat them down with the paper towel to remove any excess moisture.

3 Cook for 1 more minute if needed. Let them cool before serving.

4 Store in an airtight container for up to 3 weeks in the refrigerator or freeze.

Liver Treats

ingredients :

1 pound (.45 kg) liver

1 cup (237 ml) cornmeal

1½ cups (355 ml) wheat flour

3 tablespoons (44 ml) molasses

1 Preheat oven to 200°F (93°C).

2 Puree the liver in a blender.

3 Mix the liver with the remaining ingredients. Put the mixture in a microwave-safe dish and microwave for approximately 7 minutes.* Your goal is to dry out the liver, so that you can insert a toothpick in the middle and have it come out clean when the liver mixture is done.

4 While the mixture is still warm, cut into bite-size pieces. Place the pieces on a cookie sheet for 1½ hours at 200°F (93°C). Store in an airtight container for up to 3 weeks in the refrigerator or freeze.

When the mixture comes out of the microwave, flip it over and allow the bottom to dry out on a countertop space. The trick here is to remove as much moisture as possible from the liver mixture.

Kissable Breath

ingredients :

2¾ cups (651 ml) brown rice flour

2 tablespoons (30 ml) steel cut oats

2 teaspoons (10 ml) baking powder

2 cups (473 ml) fresh parsley

2 tablespoons (30 ml) finely chopped mint (I used dried)

¼ cup (59 ml) finely grated carrots

¼ cup (59 ml) shredded mozzarella cheese

2 tablespoons (30 ml) olive oil

1 cup (237 ml) water, give or take

1 Preheat oven to 200°F (93°C).

2 Mix flour, oats, and baking powder in a large bowl. Add parsley, mint, carrots, cheese, and oil to the dry ingredients and stir well. Gradually pour in the water a little at a time and mix until everything is well combined. The dough will need to be moist, not crumbly.

3 Lightly flour your working space and knead the dough for 2–3 minutes. Then roll out the dough until ¼" (6 mm) thick. Cut into desired shapes. Bake 20–30 minutes until biscuits begin to brown. Store in an airtight container in the refrigerator for up to 3 weeks of freeze.

Pill Pockets

ingredients :

1 tablespoon (15 ml) milk

1 tablespoon (15 ml) peanut butter

2 tablespoons (30 ml) wheat flour

1 Mix all the ingredients together in a small bowl, using a fork. Take the mixture out of the bowl and knead it in your hand. Roll the mixture between your hands to create a "snake" about 1" (25 mm) thick. Cut the rolled dough into 1" (25 mm) pieces and store in a Ziplock® bag.

2 Wrap dough pieces around the pill when giving medication. This dough makes enough for 6–8 pill pockets.

3 Store in the refrigerator for up to 1 week depending on the freshness of milk.

Stuffers 3 Ways

Frozen Peanut Butter and Banana Stuffers

ingredients :

4 ripe bananas

**½ cup (118 ml)
peanut butter**

Peel and mash the bananas. Mix with peanut butter. Stuff the mixture into hollow bones or any dog-approved chew stuffer. Freeze. Serve once frozen.

Frozen Yogurt Stuffers

ingredients :

2 ripe bananas

½ cup (118 ml) peanut butter

1 cup (236 ml) of plain yogurt

Peel and mash the bananas. Mix with peanut butter and yogurt. Stuff the mixture into hollow bones or any dog-approved chew stuffer. Freeze. Serve once frozen.

Baby Food Stuffers

ingredients :

1 jar (4 oz.) banana baby food

½ cup (118 ml) peanut butter

1 tablespoon (15 ml) honey

½ cup (118 ml) plain yogurt

In a medium bowl, combine all ingredients. Blend well. Stuff the mixture into hollow bones or any dog-approved chew stuffer. Freeze. Serve once frozen.

Peanut Butter Bones

ingredients :

2 cups (473 ml) whole wheat flour

1 tablespoon (15 ml) baking powder

1 cup (237 ml) peanut butter

1 cup (237 ml) low-fat milk

1 Preheat oven to 375°F (191°C).

2 In a bowl, combine flour and baking powder. In another bowl, mix peanut butter and milk. Add the wet mixture to the dry mixture and mix together well until it forms a dough.

3 Turn out the dough on a lightly floured surface and knead. Roll out the dough to about ¼" (6.3 mm) thickness and cut into shapes. Place on a greased baking sheet and bake for 20 minutes or until lightly brown. Cool on a rack and store in an airtight container in the refrigerator for up to 3 weeks or freeze.

Celebration Cake

ingredients :

1 egg

¼ cup (59 ml) peanut butter

¼ cup (59 ml) peanut cooking oil

1 teaspoon (5 ml) vanilla extract

⅓ cup (79 ml) carrots, shredded

1 cup (237 ml) whole wheat flour

1 teaspoon (5 ml) baking soda

1 Preheat oven to 350°F (177°C). Grease a small shaped pan or line a 6-cup (1,422 ml) muffin pan with paper liners.

2 Combine the egg, peanut butter, oil, vanilla, and honey in a large bowl. Mix well. Stir in the carrots and mix thoroughly. Sift together the flour and baking soda and fold into the carrot mixture. Spoon the cake batter into the pans.

3 Bake for 30–40 minutes depending on pan size. Let the cake cool completely.

4 For the frosting, melt peanut butter mixture in the microwave and spread evenly on cake. Decorate.

Apple Treats

ingredients :

2½ cups (591 ml) whole
wheat flour

½ cup (118 ml) cornmeal

1 apple, finely chopped
or grated

1 egg, beaten

⅓ cup (79 ml) vegetable oil

1 tablespoon (15 ml) brown
sugar

½ cup (118 ml) cold water

1 Preheat the oven to 350°F (177°C).

2 Mix flour and cornmeal together in a mixing bowl.
Add the apple, egg, oil, brown sugar, and water
until well blended.

3 Lightly flour a workspace and roll out the dough to
about ¼" (6.3 mm) thickness. Cut out treats using any
shape cookie cutter. Bake on a greased cookie sheet
for 35 minutes. Then turn the oven off and leave
the treats inside the oven for another 30–45 minutes
until crisp.

Pumpkin Pupsicles

ingredients :

1 can 100% pure pumpkin puree

1 cup (237 ml) plain yogurt

½ cup (118 ml) peanut butter

1 Blend all ingredients until smooth. Pour into ice cube trays, muffin tins, or disposable cups. Stick a dog treat bone in the middle of each treat.

2 Freeze for 12 hours, pop them out when they are frozen, and serve.

Sweet Potato Chews

ingredients :

2–3 sweet potatoes

1 tablespoon (15 ml) olive oil

1 Preheat oven to 200°F (93℃). Wash and slice sweet potatoes with the skin on to be about ⅛–¼" (3.2 mm–6.3 mm) thick.

2 Add sliced sweet potatoes and oil to a Ziplock® bag and seal. Coat sweet potatoes with oil by shaking them in the sealed bag. Place the sweet potatoes in their oil on a baking sheet. Do not overlap.

3 Bake for about 4 hours, flipping the sweet potatoes every hour. If you want them to be chewy, bake them for less time. If you want them crispy, bake them longer.

4 Store in an airtight container in the refrigerator.

Candy Cane Twist

ingredients :

3 cups (710 ml) whole wheat flour

½ cup (118 ml) powdered milk

1 cup (237 ml) chicken broth

2 large eggs (one set aside for egg wash)

1 teaspoon (5 ml) peppermint oil

Red food coloring, optional

1 Preheat oven to 350°F (177°C). Foil line a cookie sheet and spray with nonstick cooking spray. Set aside.

2 Whisk all the wet ingredients together until well combined. Add the dry ingredients next, a little at a time, stirring as you add. Mix well. Lightly flour a surface and knead dough for 2–3 minutes. Divide the dough in half, make a well in one half of the dough, and add the peppermint oil and red food coloring. Work this into the dough until desired color is achieved. Place both dough balls back into the bowl, cover, and refrigerate for 1 hour to make the dough firm.

3 Whisk the leftover egg for the wash in a small bowl. Remove the dough from the refrigerator and break small sections of equal size off and roll them between your hands to create a long skinny cylinder shape. Do this with each color of dough. Then twist the long skinny shapes together, alternating colors to create a candy cane. Dough will be somewhat sticky; this is normal. Brush each candy cane with egg wash and bake for 10–12 minutes.

Cheese Biscuits

ingredients:

½ cup (118 ml) rolled oats

2 tablespoons (30 ml) +
2 teaspoons (10 ml) butter

½ cup (118 ml) boiling water

¼ cup (59 ml) + 2 tablespoons
(29 ml) cornmeal

1 teaspoon (5 ml) sugar

1 teaspoon (5 ml) beef
bouillon granules

¼ cup (59 ml) milk

½ cup (118 ml) cheddar
cheese, shredded

1 egg, beaten

1½ cups (355 ml) whole wheat
flour

1 Preheat oven to 325°F (164°C). In a large mixing bowl, combine oats, butter, and boiling water. Let this stand for 10 minutes.

2 Stir in cornmeal, sugar, bouillon, milk, cheese, and egg. Mix in flour, ½ cup at a time, until the dough has formed. Flour a surface and knead dough until it is smooth and no longer sticky. Roll out the dough to about ¼" (6.3 mm) thickness and cut into shapes. Place shapes on a greased cookie sheet, 1" (25 mm) apart.

3 Bake 35–45 minutes until golden brown. Cheese biscuits can be stored in an airtight container for up to 3 weeks in the refrigerator or frozen. Makes about 24 biscuits depending on shape size.

St. Paddy's Clovers

ingredients :

2 cups (473 ml) rice, uncooked

2 cups (473 ml) oats

1 cup (237 ml) chicken broth

1¾ cups (414 ml) whole wheat flour

1 egg

4 tablespoons (59 ml) apple sauce

1 15oz (425 g) can spinach, drained of all water

1 tablespoon (15 ml) olive oil

1 Preheat oven to 350°F (177°C) and grease a cookie sheet.

2 Place all ingredients in a large bowl and mix well. Lightly flour a surface and roll out the dough to no more than ½" (12.8 mm) thick. Cut out shapes with a clover-themed cookie cutter. Place on greased cookie sheet. Bake for 15–20 minutes.

3 Store in an airtight container in the refrigerator for up to 3 weeks or freeze.

Minty Chicken Jerky

ingredients :

3 chicken breasts or several chicken tenders

---

2 cups (473 ml) water

---

1 tablespoon (15 ml) lemon juice

---

1 tablespoon (15 ml) dried parsley

---

1 tablespoon (15 ml) dried mint

---

1 Preheat oven to 180°F (82°C).

2 Clean the chicken and slice them into strips depending on the size of your dog. Try to remove some of the fat from the chicken. In a bowl, combine water, lemon juice, parsley, and mint. Place chicken in the bowl and allow to marinate for at least an hour.

3 Place the chicken on a cookie sheet with about ½" (12.8 mm) spacing between pieces. Place in the oven with the oven door slightly ajar to let out moisture. Cook for about 3–4 hours until the chicken is dry in appearance and texture.

4 After the chicken has cooled, store in an airtight container in the refrigerator for up to 3 weeks. Also, the recipe works great with a dehydrator appliance.

Salmon Patties

ingredients :

1 14¾ oz (418 g) can wild-caught Alaskan pink salmon

2 cups (473 ml) mashed sweet potatoes, dry mashed with no added water or milk

1 egg

¼ cup (59 ml) chopped fresh parsley

½ teaspoon (2.5 ml) baking powder

1½ cups (355 ml) whole wheat flour

1 Preheat oven to 350°F (177°C).

2 Open can of salmon and drain. Mash up and crush any bones. Break up any salmon chunks.

3 In a large bowl, stir together salmon and sweet potatoes. Add the egg, parsley, and baking powder, stir well. Sift in flour, a little at a time, stirring frequently. The dough should be like drop cookies, firm enough to handle and not very sticky. Use your hands to roll dough into ¼–½" (6.3 mm–12.7 mm) balls. Arrange them on a greased cookie sheet and press them down with your thumb or a fork. These treats will not spread, and so you can place them close together.

4 Bake for 25–30 minutes until the bottoms are golden brown or you can flip them over; cook an additional 15 minutes for a crunchier treat.

5 Store in an airtight container in the refrigerator for up to 3 weeks.

Peanut Butter & Pumpkin Treats

ingredients :

2 large eggs

½ cup (118 ml) can pure pumpkin, not pie filling

¼ cup (59 ml) peanut butter

2½ cups (591 ml) brown rice flour

Pinch of salt, optional

Drops of water, if needed

1 Preheat oven to 350°F (177°C).

2 Mix eggs, pumpkin, and peanut butter together until smooth. Add the flour and salt. Mix until the dough forms a ball. The dough should be dry and stiff. You might need to add a little water to scrape all the drier ingredients into the dough ball.

3 Lightly flour a workspace and roll out your dough to about ¼" (6.3 mm) thickness. Use any shape cookie cutter. Place shapes on a parchment-lined cookie sheet and bake for 20 minutes on one side. Flip each treat and bake for another 10–20 minutes or until dry. Let cool and serve.

4 Store in an airtight container in the refrigerator for up to 3 weeks or freeze.

Ranch Beef Bones

ingredients :

1 pound (.45 kg) lean ground beef

2 eggs, beaten

3 cups (710 ml) whole wheat flour

1 cup (236 ml) quick-cooking rolled oats

1 cup (237 ml) water

1 Preheat oven to 350°F (177°C).

2 In a blender or food processor, combine beef and beaten eggs until well blended and set aside.

3 In a large mixing bowl, combine flour and rolled oats. Gradually mix in the beef mixture with your hands until well blended. Add water and stir to form a sticky dough. Divide dough into 2 balls so that it is easy to work. Knead each dough ball on a well floured surface for about 2 minutes. Add flour as needed so that the dough is not sticky. Roll the dough out to ¼–½" (6.3 mm–12.7 mm) thickness. Cut dough into desired shapes with a cookie cutter. Place shapes on a greased baking sheet. Bake 1 hour. After they have cooled, store in the refrigerator or freeze.

Pizza! Pizza!

ingredients :

1 cup (237 ml) buckwheat flour

1 6 oz (170 g) can tomato paste

½ cup (118 ml) mozzarella cheese, shredded

1 teaspoon (5 ml) dried parsley

1 egg

1 Preheat oven to 300°F (149°C). Line a cookie sheet with parchment paper.

2 In a large bowl, mix all ingredients one at a time, mixing well after adding each item. Mix well. Lightly flour a work surface and knead dough into a ball and roll out ⅛–¼" (3.2 mm–6.3 mm) thickness. Cut dough with cookie cutter shapes and poke holes with a fork to prevent puffing. Bake for 20–25 minutes. Cool and refrigerate for up to 3 weeks or freeze.

Oatmeal Blue Bites

ingredients :

⅔ cup (158 ml) regular oatmeal

1 cup (237 ml) blueberries

1½ cups (355 ml) whole wheat flour

½ cup (118 ml) ground flaxseed

½ cup (118 ml) plain Greek yogurt

2 tablespoons (30 ml) water or more as needed

1 Preheat oven to 350°F (177°C). Turn the oatmeal into a powder using a food processor or the like and set aside. Puree the blueberries, set aside. Combine all dry ingredients in a large bowl. Fold the blueberries and yogurt into the dry ingredients amd then add 2 table-spoons or more of water to create a dough that stays together in a ball. Lightly flour a surface and roll the dough out to ¼" (6.3 mm) thickness. Cut into desired shape and place on a lightly greased cookie sheet, parchment paper, or baking mat. Bake for 20 minutes for a soft treat. For a crispier treat, flip and then continue baking for an additional 20 minutes after flipping each treat.

2 Store in an airtight container in a refrigerator for two weeks or freeze.

Cheesy Spinach

¾ cup (177 ml) whole wheat flour

──────

¾ cup (177 ml) regular oatmeal

──────

3 tablespoons cheddar cheese, grated

──────

1 cup (236 ml) frozen spinach, thawed but not drained

──────

1 tablespoon (15 ml) olive oil

──────

4 tablespoons (59 ml) water, added one at a time until desired mixture consistency

──────

1 Preheat oven to 350°F (177°C). In a bowl, combine first 5 ingredients. Then add water, one tablespoon at a time until the desired consistency is achieved. The mixture should stick together to form a ball. Using your hands, roll pinches of the mixture into small balls and place on a lightly greased cookie sheet (parchment paper or a silicon mat also can be used). Bake for 30 minutes. Let the balls cook completely before serving.

2 Store in an airtight container for up to 2 weeks or freeze. Makes about 30 small balls.

Better Beggin'

ingredients:

3 pieces cooked bacon, chopped

1 egg

½ cup (118 ml) peanut butter

¼ cup (59 ml) beef broth

1 cup (237 ml) whole wheat flour

½ cup (118 ml) regular oatmeal

1 tablespoon (15 ml) honey

1 Preheat oven to 350°F (177°C). In a medium-size bowl combine all the ingredients. Lightly flour a surface and roll out the dough to about ⅛" (3.2 mm) thickness. The dough will be sticky and a bit wet. Using a knife, cut away the uneven sides of the dough, creating a rectangle while you work the edges. Then cut strips 1" (25.4 mm) wide by 4" (102 mm) long. Wrinkle up a sheet of aluminum foil and place in the pan. This will help to support the strips in a rippled bacon appearance while they cook.

2 Bake for 20 minutes until crisp. Store in an airtight container in the refrigerator for up to 2 weeks or freeze.

Apple Pupsicles

ingredients :

1 apple, cored, seeded, and chopped

———

½ cup (118 ml) plain Greek yogurt

———

1 tablespoon (15 ml) water

———

1 Add all ingredients to a food processor and blend well. Pour mixture into freezing containers such as ice cube trays, silicon molds, or paper cups. Freeze.

2 Yields about 6 sections of a large silicon cube tray. Serve once frozen.

ACKNOWLEDGMENTS

Have you ever heard the term "Soul Dog"? I had but never gave it another thought until I met my Goldendoodle, Granger. She is my Soul Dog. Thank you Rainfield Goldendoodles for picking out the perfect member of our family. She touches my soul daily.

A special thank you goes out to my husband Byron (you are my partner in life, my idea herder) and to my son Max, for always being eager to help me in the kitchen and for telling everyone you meet about Shaggy Dog Eats. I would have never had the self-confidence to write a book without my mentor author Cym Lowell. Thank you for paving the way.

Thanks also, to my Doodle community, IDOG Labradoodle & Goldendoodle Rescue and Texas Doodle Dogs (Lynn McMullin and Toby), and my friends Tami Northrop and Elizabeth Holder, for always being my creative sounding board and biggest fans.

A big thank you to my agent, Bob Diforio, D4EO Literary Agency, and my editor and publisher, Diana Ventimiglia, Sterling Publishing Co.

Some of the amazing photographs in this book are brought to you by these creative dog lovers:

MoeCakes Photography (page 10, No-Bake Snacks)

Elizabeth Large Photography (page 28, Liver Treats)

Jenn Larios, IG@jennfreckle (page 34, Pill Pockets)

Alison Smith Story, IG@sandwichthedoodle
(page 44, Peanut Butter Bones)

Patti Livanos (page 48, Celebration Cake)

Elizabeth Holder Photography (page 50, Apple Treats)

Kem Coan Photography (page 56, Sweet Potato Chews)

Sarah Kate Photographer, (page 62, Cheese Biscuits)

Holly Eash, (pages 66 and 76, Minty Chicken Jerky
and Ranch Beef Bones)

CREDITS

Thanks to the following for their dog photos:

6 (middle left): Sina Azmoudeh with Pure Productions/IG@eb_couture; 6 (bottom left): Amanda Marie Portraits/IG@; 12: Sarah Kate Photographer/IG@ranger_doodle; 13 (far left): Sarah Kate Photographer/IG@ranger_doodle; 13 (bottom right): Lisa Franks MoeCake Photography/IG@moecakesphoto; 18 (top left): Alison Smith Story/ IG@sandwichthedoodle; 18 (bottom right): Elizabeth Large Photography/IG@ murphyandscarlet; 19: Pet Photography 4 A Cause/IG@beachbrights; 24 (top): Poco Creek Labradoodles/IG@pococreek; 24 (bottom left): Kem Coan Photography/ IG@lynnandtoby; 25: Elizabeth Large Photography/IG@murphyandscarlett; 30: Pet Photography 4 A Cause/IG@beachbrights; 31: Patti Livanos; 36: Tami Northrop/ IG@_momma_t; 37 (bottom left): Amanda Marie Portraits/IG@; 37 (bottom right): Elizabeth Holder Photography/IG@elizabethholdphotography; 46: Simply Stacy Art; 47: Amy Richards Photography/MADE in Texas Assistance Dogs; 52 (top): Amy Whitfield; 52 (bottom right): Laurie Arnold; 53: Britt Hunter/IG@jacknmolly; 60 (top left): Amy Richards Photography/MADE in Texas Assistance Dogs; 60 (top right): Elizabeth Holder Photography/IG@elizabethholdphotography; 60 (bottom left): Amy Richards Photography/MADE in Texas Assistance Dogs; 60 (bottom right): Melissa Berger; 61: Kathy Miller; 68: Patti Livanos; 69 (left): Krystal Johnson Wilson/IG@wilsondoodleduo; 69 (top right): IG@dalelowell; 69 (bottom right): MADE in Texas Assistance Dogs; 74: Elizabeth Large Photography/IG@murphyandscarlett; 75 (top): Todd Leech; 75 (bottom left): Robyn Arouty Photography/IG@kemmycoan; 75 (bottom right): Storri Wild; 82: Elizabeth Large Photography/IG@murphyandscarlett; 83: Laura Bogar/IG@bogarlaura; 90 (top): Robyn Arouty Photography/IG@robynarouty; 90 (bottom right): Mitchell Tanclo;

INDEX

ABOUT THE AUTHOR

Christy Bright is a first time author and blogger. She is a graduate of Midwestern State University and has spent most of her career in the creative sector. She is a member of the Dog Writers Association of America and a regular animal rescue contributor. When she is not in the kitchen, you can find her blogging at www.shaggydogeats.com or posting pictures of her life on Instagram @Beachbrights. Christy resides in Houston, Texas, with her husband Byron, son Max, cat Stella, and a goldendoodle diva named Granger.